Life Lessons from a Black Girl

Ebunoluwa Banjo

Presentation by *BookLeaf Publishing*

Web: www.bookleafpub.com

E-mail: info@bookleafpub.com

ISBN: 9789358369816

First edition 2023

For all the little black girls who have felt like me.

I don't write poems

I do not write poems
I never have and I never will
I do not write stories either
I write about realities
A reality that not many experience
A reality that abounds all forms of destiny
I am not here for your comfort
Or to wipe your tears
I am here for you to come face-to-face with your demons
The ones you thought could hide forever
They are on every page waiting for you
To name them
A singular reality changes everything
A single thought changes you
I repeat I do not write poems
I write about
You

She's gone

She had brown eyes that resembled the deepest
darkest oak tree
She had kinky hair that coiled at every inch
tangling her emotions in them
She had deep coffee skin that smelled like cocoa
butter
But most of all she had big beautiful lips and
when she used them to smile the whole world
would stop on its axis
She had,
Now she has deep brown eyes she wished
resembled the ocean
She has puffy straight hair which forgot its
original pattern
She has coffee skin that she wants to resemble
caramel
But now she has a smile that barely reaches her
eyes and she treats it like a stain on her face

What is love? pt 1

To be loved is expected
To be loved is returned
But I believe it is a disgusting theory
The love that you have has become
overshadowed by romance
I do not feel
A playful intelligence
A quiet wind and a gust of disgust
The idea internally fatigues me
But I love love
Truly
Wholeheartedly
Yet I make myself a fool
Again and again
What a grotesque feeling
to cry over someone you love
But I partake again and again
What a sad little life
And the constant seek for human validation
Invalidates the feeling of love I never had
A life without love seems like one for me in this
lifetime.

Dark skin

I have an unconscious love for black people
From all parts of the diaspora
Skin dark or light
Eyes brown or green
They live within me
Each time I see the epitome of joy in
black people, it makes me joyous
I feel joy
I hear joy
I know joy
We deserve joy
We deserve abundance
We deserve clarity
I love every single thing about them
I feel the most beautiful amongst a crowd with
this skin present
They bring me
Power
Love
Happiness
The thing I once thought a punishment
Is now what I find the most pride in.

6 tablets

I had a plan
and I thought it was perfect
6 tablets
1 bottle of water
1 body
It was a date
I thought it was fate
But I couldn't
so I cried until the white in my eyes
turned a blush pink
I didn't talk for 16 hours
and I sat in my bed.
There was no regret
But disappointment.
After that day
I knew I was too far gone.

Geographical fugitive

There is a definition of home in the Oxford
Dictionary
it says
the place where one lives permanently,
especially as a member of a family or household
Yet there is no permeance to my home
it changes as the sky comes up
Bringing a new dawn to everyone
My home is not a person or place
I have a British passport
But my homes have been in every country you
can think of
My home follows me
my home lives in me and I live in all of them
And when I have had my fill
I run away until I find something new
I will not be tied down
And when the places I once called mine depart
from my line of vision
I am back to the person, the place and the people
that always knew me.

What is love? pt2

Sometimes all I want to be is loved
Have someone wrapped around my finger
My hands in their hair
Looking into each other's eyes
I want to lie in a bed
No words
No actions but to stare at a future
Live
Cry
Talk
Sleep
That's a happy life
I crave a love I know I will never experience
It's a bomb
it doesn't have to be permanent
It's gonna explode
I want to be able to say goodbye
And get my heartbroken
And feel like I will never be able to breathe again
And only the wind will reach us
I want to believe in destiny
And that I have one that bares my soul
it's better than thinking I'm unlovable
And as I turn the last pages of this romance book I
can be grateful
Content
I found something in its essential form

What am I?

I am thick and black
I am so sticky I cling onto you for the rest of
your life
the only way to expunge me is to pray I don't
find you
I eat away at your soul
I drown you in my tar until your lungs are so full
You can't breathe
I will repeat this process again and again
Until you are at your ultimate lowest
and even then I will drink all the remaining
nutrients you have left
I know you as well as you know me.

Clock Tower

37,843,200 minutes
That is typically how many minutes someone
has in life
dumbed down to data
I want a life full of fulfilment
I want to spend all these minutes selfishly
I am talking about what I want but I need to
savour every single minute
Even if I don't make it to the mark
I am in a race against time
We all are
Soon these minutes will no longer have value
I used to wish I had no time left on the clock
But my clock is still churning away counting
down before it will stop
So I say
Confess
Scream
Cry
That is the beauty of the clock tower
Only you can decide what your minutes are
spent on
And finally when the clock stops churning
You can say you were limitless
and the only currency you have left is
memories.

How are you?

I am miserable
I feel as if I am failing at every single thing I put
my hand to
And I keep trying again and again to receive the
same news
I feel as if I am drowning
each time I come up for air
I suffocate a little more and one day
I know in my heart I will stop trying to fight
And give in
The ocean that I was once drowning me will
carry me
To my abyss of nothingness
But what scares me most is that I won't even try
To save myself
This is my idea of what fine means.

I threw up

My hands are shaking
I can hear the blood rushing in my head
Yet the only thing I seem to remember is
'I have never seen a girl eat so much'
And that thought sends me into a spiral
But instead of finding any sense of rational
My fingers dip further back into my throat
And my knuckles are now stained with hot
saliva
and I purge all the contents
until I feel an emptiness
until my belly enshrouded by fat feels empty
then I think if I keep up
maybe just maybe I can look in the mirror
I threw up
and it is all my fault.

Dear Happiness

It's me again
It's been a while since I last heard from you
And I know it's my fault
But I need you to know that you should not
come back
Because you
Wholeheartedly terrify me
it's your uncertainty
it's the fact that you make me feel so effortlessly
good
Then disappear as if I'm an afterthought
What makes it even worse you come back as
you see fit
leaving me to pick up what you have broken
You leave me dazed
The truth is you are selfish
and I am selfish
I want you to myself
and you just leave
so for a final time
I urge you to stay away
this is not a plea
It's a warning.
I no longer need you.

Cigarette dreams

All the people I happen to have one thing
Only one thing in common
They destroy their lungs
Hell
It is also what we have in common
While they burn themselves from the inside out
I am internally drowning
Both of my lungs are filled with water
Two polar opposite problems
That find comfort in the other
So bad that I live within my dreams
As my eyelids get heavy
and I picture them standing
They blow away
Just like the cloud of cigarette smoke
I first found them in
That is when I know
My pining is over.

To the one who taught me hatred

You have destroyed me
I am not saying this to make you seem important
But you were the catastrophe that completely
stripped me of my personhood
My sense of who I am is entangled in what you
stole from me
You owe me
My tears
My body
My childhood
You owe me every little success you make in
your life
You owe me all the hair on my head that carried
all the memories of your torment
There was a moment in time
Where I loved you with every ounce of my
being
Each mistake would be forgiven in a heartbeat
And it always will be
But I am leaving
And I am never coming back
You will not hear my forgiveness anymore
You will no longer hear my heart crying for you
to comfort me

I will leave
And all memories that lead back to you will burn
I wish you the best
But most importantly I wish you were better.

My little joy

This story is my future
I dedicate this to chubby cheeks
And big eyes that look at me for safety
I want to promise you a few things
Before I even enter that season of my life
I promise to be the best I can be
I promise to try and understand you
No matter how frustrated I am
To you my future Love
I promise to be the person you look up to
To be the mother my own refused to be
And most of all I will choose you as you choose
me
You my love
will change my entire existence.

Hello Again

Hello
I'm here again
in this place
after saying I wouldn't be back
But that doesn't piss me off
It is the fact it's the same
And I'm the same
I am in an equilibrium
but I'm here to stay
And I'm not going to fight it
not even a little.
so that's why I say
hello again.

Bathroom dates

I have sat in the room
In the same spot
In the same position
For nearly all the years of my life
It's a little paradise that contains each and all my
feelings
Each and every human emotion
Has been sucked up by this very room
And diffused into another universe
It happens to be the safety net for life,
and when I have fallen too far to the ground
you know where to find me.

What is love? pt 3

I don't think I have an answer
I never will if I'm being honest
Me and my concept of love is
Parasitic
I live off of love to move me
While love feeds off my very soul
I will give anything
And I mean anything to understand
What this concept is
But with such passion I hold
I must realise that realism plays a part in my
every fantasy
I think I have loved
But never romantically
Not because I'm so completely fretful
But I do not think my body deserves love
I don't think my brain deserves love
Hell
This little six-year-old that lives in me
Learnt love was a pain
And didn't say it back until today
I think love is to be left alone
Unfiltered
Untouched
Behind a glass cage where no one can access it

And my love will never see the light of day.
I am so sorry I failed you little me
But it's too dangerous.

3 wishes

If I was given three wishes
I would only ask for one thing
This is no selfless act
But I need one thing that will grant me my
heart's desires
I want a car
but that car carries me home
to a white picket fence
With a significant other that loves me
That spacious home contains
the sound of tiny pitter-patters
Rushing to the door
and crowding me with calf hugs
It would be noisy
it would be quiet
but it would be mine
and that wish could save
my wretched soul.

It's over

They never loved you
They loved what you could do for them
They never wanted you
Tell needed all your attention so you couldn't
move on
It's a fact of life that you refuse to believe
But the reality where you think they need you is
all in your head
It's over and that is petrifying
I understand
But you are breathing air
It's over but you still have the ability
To choose what you want
Become disillusioned
And start loving yourself
It's over
But your journey is just beginning.

To S

You annoy my very core
I have never met someone that has rattled me as
much as you do
But I owe you the person I am becoming
I owe
To you my dear
I owe my very life
You have saved me in more ways than one can
save another
And you are going to save so many along the
way
I have not always been the kindest
Or the most loving
But you love me despite my flaws
Every phone call I make to you
Makes me treasure you more and more
I love you so fucking much
It scares me
You are my soulmate in one way than one
For that, I will never forget you
I appreciate you so much
Thank you for finding me.

www.ingramcontent.com/pod-product-compliance
Lightning Source LLC
LaVergne TN
LVHW010902200726
843508LV00012B/2964